THE CA
AT
NERJA

EDICIONES
Aldeasa

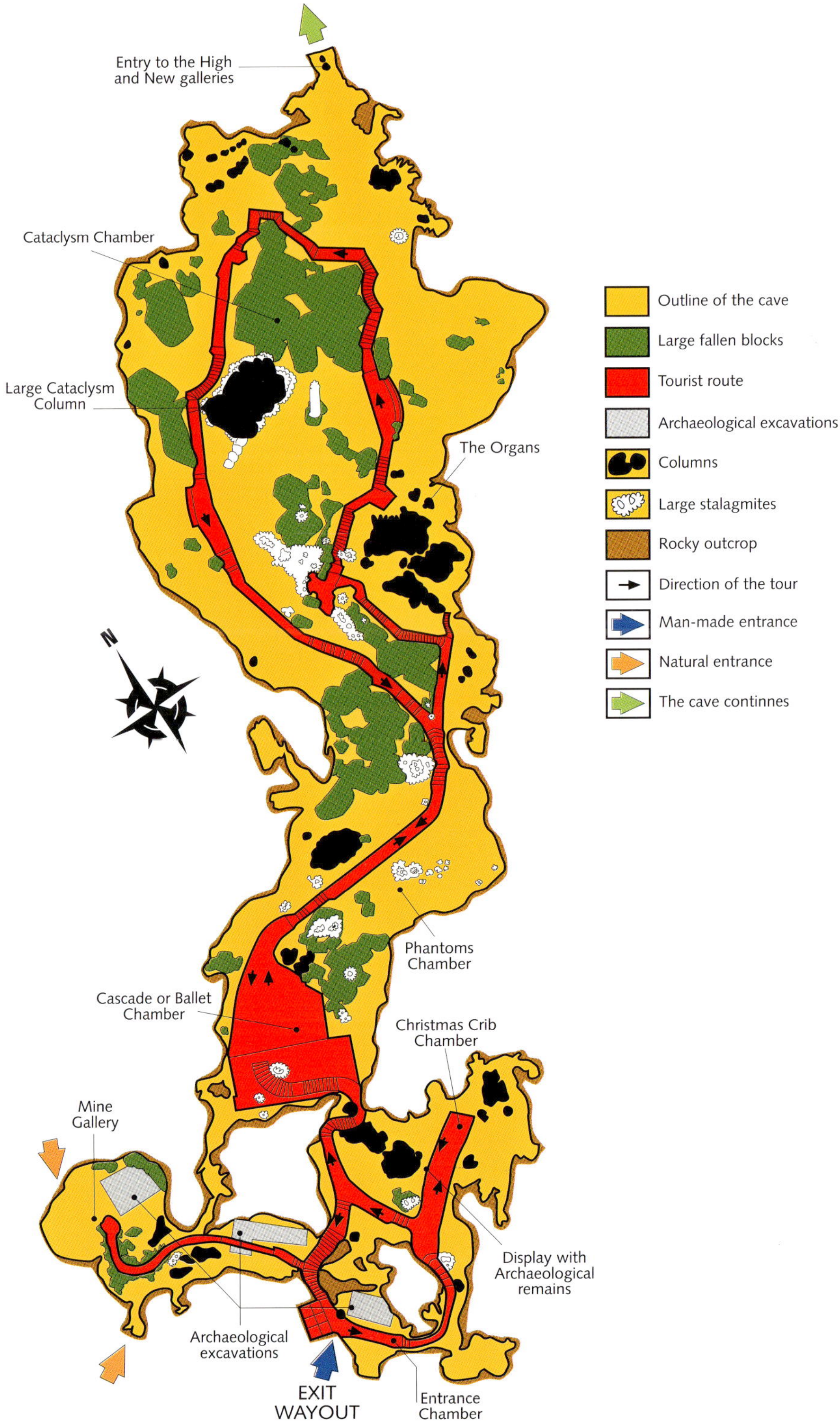

Plan of the Cave at Nerja.

THE CAVE AT NERJA

The Landscape 4

The Cave of Wonders 4

Time's Sculptures 6

The Lower or tourist Galleries 10

The Upper Galleries
and the New Galleries 18

Earlier inhabitants 20

The Paintings at Nerja 24

Glossary 30

THE LANDSCAPE

The Cave at Nerja is located on the lower slopes of the Sierra Almijara at its lowest point, a few kilometres outside the town of Nerja in the south-east of the province of Malaga. Close to the coast, the nearest village to the cave is the village of Maro, located in the area between Nerja and Almuñecar. The name Nerja derives from the Arabic "Narixa" which means a spring of water.

The landscape of this region which borders the Mediterranean is characterised by the high peaks of the mountains with their craggy slopes. Inhabited for many years by the Arabs, this terrain was traditionally a source of honey, sugar cane and various other products such as sweet wine and raisins, all of which were grown and produced locally. In addition, since ancient times when the cave was inhabited by prehistoric settlers, Nerja has been a centre for shellfish gathering.

The natural setting of the cave is formed by the rocky outcrops of the sierra and the farmed lands of the Axarquía which are cultivated in steep terraces with vines, olives and almonds, in addition to the small bays of deep and clear blue sea. The setting is completed by the so-called "white villages" of Maro, Frigliana, Torrox and Competa, perched on the slopes and peaks of the mountains of this Andalucian mountain range which looks outwards to the sea.

From the village of Maro is a view of an impressive cliff and a small bay which have been designated a Protected Natural Site due to their outstanding beauty and rich natural environment.

The Cave at Nerja is an important element in the promotion of this coastal zone of the Axarquía as a tourist destination.

THE CAVE OF WONDERS

The cave was discovered by accident in 1959 by a group of local youngsters who were catching bats for fun in the part of the cave now known as the Mine Chamber, which was at that time used as a rubbish tip. On that particular day, 11 of January, they were in the cave and noted a strong current of air rising up from a deep opening. Unaware of what was inside, they tried to get into the opening, but were defeated by the presence of solid masses of stalagmites. They therefore decided to return the next day and break them down. They eventually succeeded in entering through a narrow and extremely steep aperture which led them inside until they emerged in what is now known as the *Cataclysm Chamber*. No sooner were they inside than they found human remains which discouraged them from going any further. On returning home, the youngsters related what they had found, but it was only a few days later that a photographer and a doctor decided to go inside. Eventually the discovery was officially announced by the press.

The village of Maro facing the Mediterranean. View from the Cave at Nerja.

The exceptional nature of the cave encouraged the construction of a visitors' entrance in 1960 and the cave was initially given the name of the Cave of Wonders. The Committee for Archaeological Excavation of Malaga was responsible for this, and also started work on locating an easier entrance into the cave for experts and the general public than the one found by the youngsters. After investigating various galleries, a new entrance was discovered four metres underground just by the root of an old sabine tree which led into one of the cavities. The next step was to break through the rock which had made the entrance impassible. At the same time, work started on restoration and improvements to the cave to facilitate the initial investigations by archaeologists and geologists.

The Cave at Nerja was declared an Artistic Historical Monument on 15 June 1961. The youngsters who discovered it were awarded with the creation of stone sculpture commemorating their discovery which was placed at the entrance to the cave.

From then on until the present day the Cave at Nerja has been the subject of continuous excavations and detailed scientific investigation relating to its ecology, geological origins and prehistoric past. The campaigns carried out to date have fully opened up the structure and revealed not just the *Lower* or *Tourist Galleries,* but also the *Upper Galleries,* discovered in 1959, and the *New Galleries* which were unknown until the 1970s.

The enormous interest in this natural monument is clear from the thousands of visitors who visit every year in order to admire the marvellous galleries made up of stalactites, stalagmites and other calceous formations. Every visitor to the Cave at Nerja is a witness to an astonishing natural process in which those patient architects, time and water erosion, have been at work for 5 million years.

It is also worth emphasising the importance of the cave as a significant repository of archaeological remains and cave art from the Western Mediterranean prehistoric period.

The Cave at Nerja forms one of a group with other Andalucian caves such as those at La Pilota, Doña Trinidad and Navarro, whose walls were painted during the Paleolithic age.

TIME'S SCULPTURES

The Cave at Nerja is of the so-called karst type. Its formation dates back to the Pliocenic and Pliostocenic periods, around 5 million years ago. The marbles of the Sierra in which it is located were "carved out" many years before that, 200 million years ago during the Triassic period, from the deposits of calcareous mud in shallow waters.

The process which gave rise to the origin and shape of the cave is known as karstification combined with neo-tectonic activity (the movement of the earth's crust).

Column formations *(detail).* The Christmas Crib Chamber, Lower Galleries.

From this process derives the description of the cave as a karstic cavity. Karstification is fundamentally rain water erosion through filtration. Gradually these infiltrations of water dissolve the calcium-magnesic carbonate of the marbles, creating fissures and conduits which produce the calciferous cavities.

It was during the periods of warm climate in the Quarternary that the accumulation of calcium carbonate deposits produced a wide variety of solid formations in the inside of the cave such as stalactites, stalagmites, columns, carpets, flags and defiles, collectively known as speleothems. The cave has almost every type of these features currently known and it is therefore not surprising that the Cave at Nerja is considered outstanding among European caves of this type. We should emphasise that this karstification process is still ongoing, as the cave is located above the water table level and therefore continues to receive filtrations from nearby springs. The nearest spring to the cave is the one at Maro.

The cave measures 7,219.38 metres from North to South, and the approximate volume of all its chambers and galleries is about 264,379.33 cubic metres. Only around one-third of these areas are currently open to the general public. The cave currently has three entrances: the one created artificially in 1960 which is today used for tourist visits, and the two natural ones.

Inside, the area can be divided into two quite distinct zones: the area open for tourist visits, known as the Lower Galleries, and the Upper and New Galleries. These latter areas are closed to the public (although it is possible to visit them on Saturday mornings in small groups, wearing suitable clothes and after some initial preparation).

THE LOWER OR TOURIST GALLERIES

The entrance to the underground area is set in a botanical garden with pines and typical plants such as bougainvillea, and features the monument set up to the young people who discovered the cave. The facilities at the entrance include the Information Centre which has been created to provide additional information during visits, both on the Cave and the Foundation. It has an educational exhibition and various additional facilities (an audiovisual room, a shop, restaurant and car park) for the visitor. The route through the various chambers only covers around one third of the whole area of the cave.

The Lower or Tourist Galleries consist of seven chambers known as the *Entrance Chamber*, the *Christmas Crib Chamber*, the *Elephant's Tusk Chamber*, the *Cascade or Ballet Chamber*, the *Phantoms Chamber*, the *Cataclysm Chamber* and finally, on our way back near the entrance, the *Cavern Chamber* and the *Mine Chamber*. These chambers are surprisingly large, with huge ceilings inhabited by the features such as stalactites, stalagmites, flags, defiles and

The Pineapple. Speleothem. Chamber of the Levels. Upper Galleries.
Previous double-page spread: The entrance into the Phantoms Chamber. Lower Galleries.

other geological phenomena which we mentioned earlier.

The subtle and theatrical illumination brings out the large numbers of shapes, forms and outlines created by the natural formations within the caves. Their unique shapes have been interpreted in numerous different ways and the names which they have been given are the result of visitors' imaginative interpretations.

A descending staircase leads us to the first stage of the itinerary: the Entrance Chamber. Here we will encounter an important archaeological find of ceramics and utensils displayed in a case alongside explanatory text panels.

Our route is marked out on the ground with arrows, and continues along a narrow passageway cut out of the rock which leads into the Chamber of the Christmas Crib, a space consisting of a vaulted corridor faced with formations of columns, defiles and stalactites. Equally noteworthy is the display case with the remains of an 8,300-year-old burial of a woman aged around 18-20 who, as a point of interest, died from acute otitis.

Nearby are the Cavern Chamber and the Mine Chamber, which feature part of the natural entranceway to the cave and where archaeological investigations are currently in process. For this reason these areas are currently closed to the public.

Climbing up some steps we reach the Elephant's Tusk Chamber, so named because the fossilised tree trunk covered in stalagmitic material looks like a tusk. A narrow passage connects this room with the viewing area in the top part of the Ballet or Cascade Chamber. The amazing gours in the form of a cascade give this chamber its name.

The hemicyclical shape of this room and its resonant acoustics make it an ideal natural setting for performances. Since its discovery it has been used to house the International Festival of the Cave at Nerja. Every summer concerts, ballet performances, classical dance and flamenco are performed with great success. When the cave was officially opened in 1960, the French company "La Tour de Paris" performed Tchaikovsky's "Swan Lake", the first time such an event had ever been held in a cave. The auditorium, located on a natural platform created by the Cascade Chamber, holds 600 spectators. Prehistoric vessels and utensils have also been found here.

The itinerary continues once we have gone past a large column known as "The Boot", situated in the centre of the Phantoms Chamber with its fantastical and varied stalagmites. This chamber narrows at the end with a mass of rocks and great blocks of stalactites which create various "architectural" features, such as the one known as "The Castle".

The route continues in some of the lowest areas of the cave which features every imaginable type of formation. This is the Cataclysm Chamber. Today it appears as a great subterranean space with huge and disordered fragments of calcified rock, the

The Castle. Stalagmite formation. The Cataclysm Chamber, Lower Galleries. *Pages 12-13:* Vaults and floors of Stalactites and Stalagmites. Both in the Cataclysm Chamber, Lower Galleries.

result of the earthquakes which took place in the cave. During prehistoric times this chamber was used for group burials.

The Cataclysm Chamber is more than 100 metres long, 50 metres wide and extends in places to a height of more than 30 metres. A viewing platform allows us to appreciate its huge scale, emphasised by the presence of the Great Column, the largest known to date (32 metres high with a base measuring 13 x 7m). From investigations in this chamber it has been possible to date the earthquake which took place in this chamber to 800,000 years ago. In addition, the visitor will note large blocks which have come away from the ceiling in the form of sloping stalactites and from which vertical formations are still growing.

Leaving the viewing area and going down the steps we pass near to The Organs – formations created by very large folds in the walls.

The various shapes which the water has sculpted from the rocks bring to mind particular characters, such as the one known as "Pinocchio" or "Cyrano de Bergerac". This is situated behind the Great Column in the Cataclysm Chamber and is one of the most popular visitor attractions at the Cave.

Having left the Cataclysm balcony, we go down a series of steps to the area known as The Bridge. From here we can make out the steep and challenging passage that leads to the galleries known as the Upper and New Galleries. It is unlikely that a way through will be made for the general public, as this would involve destroying the natural surroundings, in contrast to the entry created into the Lower Galleries which was created without damaging or altering the outside of the cave.

The route back begins once we have gone around the Great Column and, in the reverse direction to our initial route, return to the Phantoms Chamber and the Cascade Chamber. The route back allows for new and different views of the various chambers.

Finally, we once again pass close to the primeval entrances to the Mine Chamber and the Cavern Chamber and climb up the final staircase, completing our tour.

THE UPPER GALLERIES AND THE NEW GALLERIES

A narrow passage located at the top of the far south-east end of the Cataclysm Chamber is the entrance to the area not generally open to the public. These are the Upper Galleries, discovered by chance in 1959, and the New Galleries, which were unknown until 1969 and 1970 and discovered following detailed study of the cave.

These chambers are larger and even more remarkable than those we have already seen, due to the richness and variety of the speleothems and the underwater formations, as well as the wide variety of cave paintings. Together they form a series of huge rooms with steep entrances, separated by a rocky mass and a jumble of great blocks and walls of various stone formations.

Pinocchio or Cyrano de Bergerac, Stalagmite formation. Lower Galleries.
Pages 16-17: Flags, Chamber of the Levels. New Galleries.

The route through these areas is so labyrinthine that the visitor can easily become lost here.

The difficult access to the Upper Galleries is through a series of corridors which cross three, small transitional galleries known as the *Kitchen Chamber,* the *Fish Chamber* and the *Labyrinths Chamber.* These lead on to four large chambers: the *Columns of Hercules Chamber,* which measures about 90 x 40 metres and whose wall paintings show that prehistoric man had already discovered this space; the *Immensity Chamber,* whose name pays tribute to its huge dimensions of 135 x 95 metres; and, on the south side, the *Gallery of the Levels,* which has great groups of stalagmites and water-level crystallisations. Some of these are known as Pineapples as their outline is surprisingly similar to that of the fruit. A huge stalactite which has fallen from the roof and buried itself in the floor gives this space the name of the *Lance Chamber,* an area whose dimensions are larger than those of the Cascade Chamber, the Phantoms Chamber and the Cataclysm Chamber combined. This gallery offers one of the finest views of any of the spaces whithin the cave.

Moving on, we come to the last and largest of the rooms: the *Mountain Chamber.* With a volume of 64,804.90 cubic metres, its main feature is the huge blocks strewn about the centre. Here we find the famous "Nails", calciferous layers covering small splinters of rock which look like finger nails, hence their nickname.

EARLIER INHABITANTS

From the time of its discovery in 1959, the cave has been the object of numerous archaeological campaigns whose results have revealed the nature of this prehistoric find. In addition, they have yielded much information on when it was occupied in its various functions as a living place, sanctuary and burial ground. It is known that it was occupied for a total of 25,000 years and that it was subsequently sealed up for around 4,000 years until it was rediscovered. The most important archaeological discoveries have been found in the early entrance, in the Mine, Cavern and Entrance chambers.

The most recent investigations have revealed a continuous presence of prehistoric cultures from the beginning of the upper Paleolithic period until the Copper Age. It would seem that the last peoples to inhabit the cave were hunter-gatherers and fishermen. Their surviving testimony is the impressive corpus of cave paintings comprising more than 600 painted and engraved motifs on the walls, applied in large numbers during the Paleolithic period as well as in later periods.

Other remains of these inhabitants include fragments of ceramic, marble bracelets, underground stores and human remains. The remains were found in group burials in the Cataclysm, Phantoms, Ballet, Cavern and Mine chambers, as well as what is now the entranceway to the cave. All of these, together with the major group of paintings, allow us to piece together, or at

Nails. Speleothems. Mountain Chamber. New Galleries.

least have some idea, of how these prehistoric groups lived.

The periods of occupation began in the Upper Paleolithic era, 27,000 years ago. The small number of implements found belong to the Paleolithic culture of the Aurignacian period.

Burials from the Solutrian culture dating between 18,000 and 14,000 BC indicate a group of hunter-gatherers. Also dating from this period is the Sanctuary with the cave paintings in the Lower and Upper Galleries referred to earlier. The first bone fish hooks belong to the Magdalenian culture, between 14,000 and 10,000 BC have been recorded here, while the so called fish-form paintings also belong to this period. Stones decorated with geometric designs have also been located in this level.

One of the most interesting aspects of the culture of the cave inhabitants during the Magdalenian and Post-Magdalenian periods (ca.12,000 BC) is the diet of shellfish, which was gathered with increasing skill.

The prehistoric men of Nerja were the clear forerunners of the present culture which still continues with the traditional fishing methods.

The Epipaleolithic, dating from12,000 to 9,000 BC, is fully represented by a series of engraving tools, graters and painted stones. Found in the Christmas Crib Chamber was the grave mentioned above of a woman aged around 18 and dating from this period.

From between 7,000 and 4,800 BC, during the Neolithic period, we have remains of an organised human group. Towards the room open to the public the occupation of the cave widens out. Here archaeologists have identified the inhabitants' feeding habits, with a diet consisting mainly of different fruits from the area, as well as the presence of domestic animals such as dogs, goats and sheep. In addition, piece of ceramic, tools and a number of ornaments and jewels have been found.

The graves from this period have been found in the Cascade, Phantoms and Cataclysm chambers. The burials in the Cavern and Mine chambers date from the Chalcolithic or Copper Age, 2,000 years ago.

Other equally interesting remains from this period are the arrows and objects such as weights for the loom which provide evidence for primitive textile manufacture, and a more elaborate eating service.

Around 2,000 BC water swept rocks and sediment into the cave and it closed up permanently until it was rediscovered in 1959.

THE PAINTINGS AT NERJA

Cave paintings are found throughout the site, both on the walls and on the stalagmites. While the prehistoric artists were more active in the Lower Galleries, they also produced interesting work in the Upper ones.

These paintings have been the subject of exhaustive research by specialists.

Fish-form motifs. Cave painting in red. Chamber of the Fish, Upper Galleries.
Pages 22-23: Entrance to the Lance Chamber. New Galleries.

The Organs Chamber features a drawing of a deer, while the Cascade Chamber has a clearly defined outline of an Iberian goat.

The largest grouping of Paleolithic drawings is to be found in the so-called Solutrian Sanctuary, where the paintings can be dated to this culture and also correspond to other groups of Mediterranean cave paintings of this date. The designs include a wide variety of animals (deer, goats and other four-footed animals), as well as symbols, all of which were executed in black and red. This sanctuary occupied the Lower as well as the Upper Galleries.

The Magdalenian "chapel" or Fish Chamber is equally interesting, located in the Upper Galleries. This consists of a two-metre square space whose surface is divided into panels by the fish motifs mentioned earlier, all drawn in red. Some experts have identified the creatures depicted as dolphins, but it is more likely that they are seals which are very abundant in this region. It seems likely that these motifs followed a pre-conceived decorative design or programme which became increasingly complex from one area to another. Some appear in areas which are difficult to reach, which is also interesting. The compositional and technical coherence of these drawings makes it possible to suggest that they were all executed by one hand.

Other anthropomorphic paintings and engraved motifs in red as well as various black signs have also survived from the Postpaleolithic and Neolithic periods, as well as the Chalcolithic.

These schematic engravings which form a sort of decorative frieze, are located in the Cavern Chamber and have been interpreted as dance scenes. Interlaced motifs have also been found in the Upper Galleries, while in the Cataclysm and Kitchen chambers, which together form the so-called Labyrinth, are double triangular engravings which have been interpreted as female "idols".

An Iberian goat has been identified in the Chamber of the Columns of Hercules, painted on a stalactite. This has clearly defined outlines, formed from thick black lines combined with a red which has faded over time.

With regard to technique and materials, these paintings were painted on the walls of the cave with some implement or with the fingers. The colours used were natural vegetable or organic pigments, for example, iron oxide for the yellow and red, and manganese or wood charcoal for the black.

The presence of these paintings provides key evidence regarding which areas of the cave were occupied, while they are also highly significant within the overall context of European cave painting.

Iberian Goat. Cave painting in black. Chamber of the Columns of Hercules. Upper Galleries. *Pages 26-27:* Column known as The Boot and vault with stalactites. Cascade or Ballet Chamber, Lower Galleries.

GLOSSARY

Calcite: a mineral sediment which forms stalactites, stalagmites and other crystalline formations by process of precipitation.

Defiles: crystalline aggregates formed from the precipitation of calcium carbonate over large surface areas.

Flags: crystalline aggregates in the form of undulating drapery resembling waving flags.

Folds: a geological phenomenon which results in folds or creases in the rock due to the compression of the earth.

Columns: crystalline aggregates formed by stalactites which fuse with stalagmites to form a column.

Karst: calcareous terrain which decomposes during to the action of atmospheric agents and the dissolution of surface waters, resulting in irregular formations such as crests, cracks, depressions and caverns.

Magdalenian: a pre-historic culture at the end of the Upper Paleolithic period.

Pineapples: crystalline aggregates in bizarre shapes which form in areas where there is most water

Solutrian: a prehistoric, cultural period of the Upper Paleolithic era characterised by pieces of regularly carved flint, needles, bone punches, sculptures and cave paintings. It corresponds to the Homo sapiens sapiens period between 18,000 and 14,000 years before the present.

Speleothems: stalactites, stalagmites, defiles, flags and other crystalline aggregates formed by the precipitation of calcium carbonate.

Stalactites: crystalline aggregate of fibrous and concentric structure which gives rise to the formation of hanging conical body of variable dimensions. Frequently found inside caves hanging from a fissure in the roof and created by dripping water and calcium carbonate.

Stalagmite: crystalline aggregate of various forms arranged in concentric layers and formed by the juxtaposition of calcium carbonate. They usually appear on the floor of caves below stalactites due to the accumulation of liquid which these give out.

Christmas Crib Chamber *(detail).*

© ALDEASA, 2004
I.S.B.N.: 84-8003-429-7
D. L.: M-14490-2004
Photographs: © Fundación Cueva de Nerja
© Agapito Sanchidrián Torti
© Pedro Garrido
(Front cover, p. 11, p. 21)

Front cover: Detail of the Cataclysm Chamber.
Lower Galleries.
Back cover: View of the village of Maro.
Produced and Published by: ALDEASA
Text: Ana López del Hierro
Translation: Laura Suffield
Collection design: A. Ochoa de Zabalegui
Layout: Myriam López Consalvi
Film makers: Lucam
Printers: Estudios Gráficos Europeos